25th Anniversary
Celebration

by
Pamela Conn Beall and
Susan Hagen Nipp

illustrated by
Nancy Spence Klein

PSS!
PRICE STERN SLOAN

A special thanks to all who
have helped us reach this
25th anniversary

Printed on recycled paper

Cover illustration by Lisa Guida

Typesetting and engraving by Sherry Macy
Lines, Curves & Dots Graphics

Copyright © 2002 by Pamela Conn Beall and Susan Hagen Nipp.
Published by Price Stern Sloan, a division of Penguin Putnam Books
for Young Readers, 345 Hudson Street, New York, NY 10014.

ISBN: 0-8431-7757-8

B C D E F G H I J

PREFACE

Wee Sing celebrates its 25th anniversary! We can hardly believe so many years have passed since we began collecting and writing songs for children. Twenty-five years ago as young mothers and former music teachers it was difficult to find a good collection of traditional children's songs. So, we decided to create our own—and *Wee Sing* was born. From the beginning, our intent has been to preserve favorite songs that have been passed down for generations. In sharing them, we hope they will be passed on to future generations.

Recognizing that music is so valuable to the growth and development of children, we have continued to add to *Wee Sing*'s collection of books, audios, and videos. When traditional songs aren't found for a particular subject area, such as dinosaurs, we write original songs to fill that void.

Over the years, it has been a joy to watch *Wee Sing* spread, not only across the United States, but around the world. Occasionally, the lyrics and text have been translated, but more often, *Wee Sing* is being used as a vehicle for teaching English as a second language.

Choosing which songs to include in this special edition was difficult since we could only include 46 from the hundreds of songs in the *Wee Sing* collection. Our choices needed to represent a wide variety of themes, appeal to various ages, and have historical significance. The favorites that couldn't be included in this collection can still be found in one of the many books in the *Wee Sing* series.

Thank you for joining in our *Wee Sing 25th Anniversary Celebration*. We hope you will sing and share these traditional favorites with today's children. In the meantime, our journey continues.

Pam Beall
Susan Nipp

TABLE OF CONTENTS

The More Wee Sing Together 6
If You're Happy 7
Skidamarink 8
Bingo 10
Do Your Ears Hang Low? 11
The Big Rock Candy Mountains 12
Down by the Bay 14
Six Little Ducks 15
Row, Row, Row Your Boat 16
Head and Shoulders 17
Dry Bones 18
Looby Loo 20
Eentsy, Weentsy Spider 22
Baby Bumblebee 23
The Ants Go Marching 24
The Bear Went Over the Mountain 26
I Love the Mountains 27
She'll Be Comin' Round the Mountain 28
John Jacob Jingleheimer Schmidt 30
Take Me Out to the Ball Game 31
To Market, to Market 32
This Little Pig Went to Market 33
Old MacDonald Had a Farm 34
Pease Porridge Hot 36
Playmate 37
My Aunt Came Back 38
Tingalayo 40
Down by the Station 41
I've Been Working on the Railroad 42
Ten in a Bed 44
The Farmer in the Dell 45
Kookaburra 46
Pop! Goes the Weasel 47
Polly Wolly Doodle 48
Hickory, Dickory, Dock 50
Ring Around the Rosy 51
The Hokey Pokey 52
Teddy Bear 53

Who Built the Ark? 54
Rain, Rain, Go Away 56
There Is Thunder 56
It's Raining 57
Sing-a-ling 58
He's Got the Whole World 59
Hush, Little Baby 60
Twinkle, Twinkle, Little Star 61

Index 62

THE MORE WEE SING TOGETHER

Traditional

The more Wee Sing to - geth - er, to -
geth - er, to - geth - er, The more Wee Sing to -
geth - er, the hap - pi - er we'll be, For
your friends are my friends, and my friends are
your friends, The more Wee Sing to -
geth - er, the hap - pi - er we'll be.

Suggestion:
During the phrase, "For your friends are my friends and my
friends are your friends," replace the words with the names of
family members or friends (for example, "There's Mother and
Father and Susie and Sammy . . . .").

IF YOU'RE HAPPY

Traditional

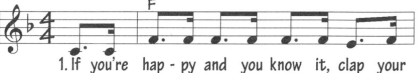

1. If you're hap-py and you know it, clap your

hands. *(clap, clap)* If you're hap-py and you

know it, clap your hands. *(clap, clap)* If you're hap-py and you

know it, then your face will sure-ly show it. If you're

hap-py and you know it, clap your hands. *(clap, clap)*

2. . . . **stomp your feet** *(stomp, stomp)* . . .

3. . . . **shout, "Hurray!"** *(Hurray!)* . . .

4. . . . **do all three** *(clap, clap, stomp, stomp, Hurray!)* . . .

Suggestion:
Make up verses and actions for other emotions (for example, sad, excited, angry . . . .).

SKIDAMARINK

Traditional

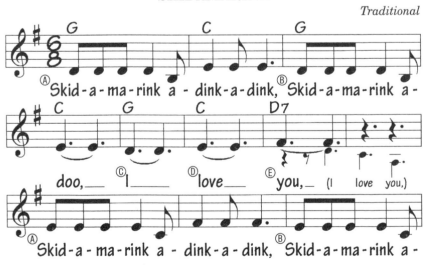

Ⓐ Skid-a-ma-rink a - dink-a-dink, Ⓑ Skid-a-ma-rink a -

doo,__ Ⓒ I__ Ⓓ love__ Ⓔ you,__ (I love you,)

Ⓐ Skid-a-ma-rink a - dink-a-dink, Ⓑ Skid-a-ma-rink a -

8

Action:

Ⓐ Right elbow in left hand, wiggle right fingers
Ⓑ Left elbow in right hand, wiggle left fingers
Ⓒ Point to self
Ⓓ Hug self
Ⓔ Point to other person
Ⓕ Arms form circle above head, lean left
Ⓖ Keep circle above head, stand straight
Ⓗ Keep circle above head, lean right
Ⓘ Sweep arms down and form new circle above head

BINGO

Traditional

1. There was a farm-er had a dog and Bin-go was his name-o. B - I - N - G - O, B - I - N - G - O, B - I - N - G - O, and Bin-go was his name-o.

2. ... *(Clap)*-I-N-G-O ...
3. ... (X)-(X)-N-G-O ...
4. ... (X)-(X)-(X)-G-O ...

5. ... (X)-(X)-(X)-(X)-O ...
6. ... (X)-(X)-(X)-(X)-(X) ...

DO YOUR EARS HANG LOW?
(Tune: Turkey in the Straw)

Traditional

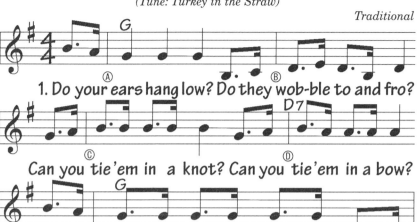

1. Do your ears hang low? Do they wob-ble to and fro?

Can you tie 'em in a knot? Can you tie 'em in a bow?

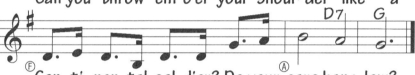

Can you throw 'em o'er your shoul-der like a

Con-ti-nen-tal sol-dier? Do your ears hang low?

2. Yes, my ⒜ears hang low and they ⒝wobble to and fro,
I can ©tie 'em in a knot, I can ⒟tie 'em in a bow,
I can ⒠throw 'em o'er my shoulder like a ⒡Continental soldier,
Yes, my ⒜ears hang low.

3. Do your ⒢ears hang high? Do they ⒣reach up to the sky?
Are they ①curly when they're wet? Are they ⒥shaggy when
they're dry?
Can you ⒠throw 'em o'er your shoulder like a ⒡Continental
soldier?
Do your ⒢ears hang high?

4. Yes, my ⒢ears hang high . . . .

Action:
⒜ Backs of hands on ears,
fingers down
⒝ Sway fingers
© Tie large knot in air
⒟ Draw bow in air with both hands
⒠ Throw both hands over
left shoulder
⒡ Salute
⒢ Hands by ears, fingers up
⒣ Arms up
① Wiggle fingers around head
⒥ Flap hands at sides of head

11

THE BIG ROCK CANDY MOUNTAINS

Traditional, Adapted

1. In the Big Rock Can - dy Moun - tains, There's a land that's fair and bright, Where the good - ies grow on bush - es, And you sleep out ev - 'ry night, Where friends are all a - round us, And the sun shines ev - 'ry day, Oh, I'm bound to go where there is - n't an - y

C **F** **C** **F**

snow, Where the rain does-n't fall and the wind does-n't

C **G7** **C**

blow, In the Big Rock Can - dy Moun - tains.

Chorus

G7 **C**

Oh, the buz-zin' of the bees in the pep-per-mint

F **C**

trees, Round the so - da wa - ter foun - tains, ___

G7 **C**

Where the lem - on - ade springs and the blue - bird

G7 **C**

sings, In the Big Rock Can - dy Moun - tains.

2. In the Big Rock Candy Mountains,
   You never change your socks,
   And little streams of lemonade
   Come a-tricklin' down the rocks,
   The critters there are friendly,
   It's such a lovely sight,
   There's a lake of stew and soda, too,
   You can paddle all around 'em in a big canoe,
   In the Big Rock Candy Mountains.
   (Chorus)

13

DOWN BY THE BAY

Traditional

1. Down by the bay____ Where the wa-ter-mel-ons grow,____ Back to my home,____ I dare not go,____ For if I do,____ My moth-er will say,____ "Did you ev - er see a snake bak-ing a cake?" Down by the bay.

2. . . . "Did you ever see a frog
   walking his dog?" . . .

3. . . . "Did you ever see a mouse
   painting his house?" . . .

Suggestion:
Continue by making up your own rhyming verses (for example, a bear combing his hair, a bee with a sunburned knee, a moose kissing a goose . . . .) and taking turns singing the solo part.

SIX LITTLE DUCKS

Traditional

1. Six lit-tle ducks that I once knew,

Fat ones, skin-ny ones, fair ones, too. But the

one lit-tle duck with the feath-er on his back,

He led the oth-ers with a quack, quack, quack!

Quack, quack, quack, quack, quack, quack!

He led the oth-ers with a quack, quack, quack!

2. Down to the river they would go,
Wibble wobble, wibble wobble, to and fro,
But the one little duck with the feather on his back,
He led the others with a quack, quack, quack!
Quack, quack, quack, quack, quack, quack!
He led the others with a quack, quack, quack!

3. Home from the river they would come,
Wibble wobble, wibble wobble, ho-hum-hum . . . .

15

ROW, ROW, ROW YOUR BOAT
(Round)

E. O. Lyte

Row, row, row your boat Gent-ly down the

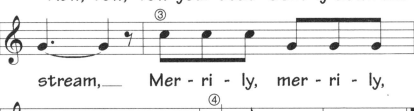

stream,___ Mer - ri - ly, mer - ri - ly,

mer-ri-ly, mer-ri-ly, Life is but a dream.___

16

HEAD AND SHOULDERS

Traditional

Head and shoul-ders, knees and toes, knees and toes,

Head and shoul-ders, knees and toes, knees and toes,____

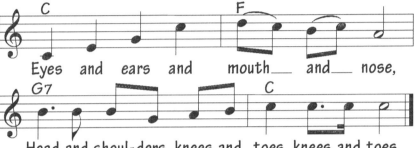

Eyes and ears and mouth____ and____ nose,

Head and shoul-ders, knees and toes, knees and toes.

Action:
Touch the different parts of the body when singing about them.

Suggestion:
* Repeat the song, omitting the word *head* throughout, but do the action.
* Repeat again, omitting *head and shoulders* throughout, but do the actions.
* Continue as above until silently doing all the actions.

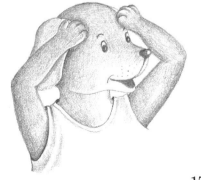

DRY BONES

Traditional

E - ze-kiel cried, "Dem dry bones!" E - ze-kiel cried, "Dem

dry bones!" E - ze-kiel cried, "Dem dry bones!" Oh, hear the

word of the Lord. The foot bone con-nect-ed to the leg bone,

The leg bone con-nect-ed to the knee bone, The knee bone con-

nect-ed to the thigh bone, The thigh bone con-nect-ed to the

back - bone, The back-bone con-nect-ed to the neck

bone, The neck bone con-nect-ed to the head bone, Oh,

hear the word of the Lord! Dem bones, dem bones gon-na

walk a-roun', Dem bones, dem bones, gon-na

walk a-roun', Dem bones, dem bones gon-na walk a-roun', Oh,

hear the word of the Lord. The head bone con-nect-ed to the

neck bone, The neck bone con-nect-ed to the back-bone, The

back-bone con-nect-ed to the thigh bone, The

thigh bone con-nect-ed to the knee bone, The

knee bone con-nect-ed to the leg bone, The leg bone con-

nect-ed to the foot bone, Oh, hear the word of the Lord!

LOOBY LOO

Here we go Loo-by Loo,_ Here we go Loo-by Light,_
Here we go Loo-by Loo,_ All on a Sat-ur-day night._

1. You put your right hand in,_____ You
put your right hand out,_ You give your right hand a
shake, shake, shake, And turn your-self a - bout. Oh,

(Chorus after each verse)

2. . . . left hand . . .
3. . . . right foot . . .
4. . . . left foot . . .
5. . . . head . . .
6. . . . whole self . . .

Formation:
Children stand in a circle, holding hands.

Action:
- Children circle around on the chorus.
- On the verses, they stop circling and do the actions by putting hand, foot, etc. inside, then outside, then back inside the circle.

EENTSY, WEENTSY SPIDER

Traditional

Ⓐ The een-tsy, ween-tsy spi-der went up the wa-ter-spout. Ⓑ Down came the rain and Ⓒ washed the spi-der out. Ⓓ Out came the sun and Ⓔ dried up all the rain, And the Ⓐ een-tsy, ween-tsy spi-der went up the spout a-gain.

Action:

- Ⓐ Make circles out of thumbs and forefingers, put circles together, twist upward
- Ⓑ Wiggle fingers while moving downward
- Ⓒ Push outward
- Ⓓ Make big circle with arms over head
- Ⓔ Hands in front, palms up, move up in rhythm

BABY BUMBLEBEE

Traditional

Ⓐ I'm bring-ing home a ba-by bum-ble-bee,

Won't my mom-my be so proud of me? I'm bring-ing home a

ba-by bum-ble-bee, Ⓑ OUCH! It stung me!

Action:
Ⓐ Cup one hand over the other
Ⓑ Throw hands open

THE ANTS GO MARCHING

(Tune: When Johnny Comes Marching)

Traditional

1. The ants go march-ing one by one, Hur-rah, Hur-rah, The ants go march-ing one by one, Hur-rah, Hur-rah, The ants go march - ing one by one, The lit-tle one stops to suck his thumb And they all go march-ing Down to the ground To get out of the rain, Boom! Boom! Boom!

2.   . . . two by two . . . tie his shoe . . .
3.   . . . three by three . . . climb a tree . . .
4.   . . . four by four . . . shut the door . . .
5.   . . . five by five . . . take a dive . . .
6.   . . . six by six . . . pick up sticks . . .
7.   . . . seven by seven . . . pray to heaven . . .
8.   . . . eight by eight . . . shut the gate . . .
9.   . . . nine by nine . . . check the time . . .
10. . . . ten by ten . . . say, *"THE END!"*

THE BEAR WENT OVER THE MOUNTAIN

(Tune: For He's a Jolly Good Fellow)

Traditional

1. The bear went o - ver the moun - tain, The bear went o - ver the moun-tain, The bear went o - ver the moun - tain, To see what he could see.

Chorus

To see what he could see, To see what he could see,

2. The other side of the mountain,
   The other side of the mountain,
   The other side of the mountain,
   Was all that he could see.

Chorus:
   Was all that he could see,
   Was all that he could see . . . .

D.C.:
   The other side of the mountain . . . .

26

I LOVE THE MOUNTAINS

(Round)

Traditional

Boom - de - ah - da, boom - de - ah - da,

Boom - de - ah - da, boom - de - ay.

① I love the moun-tains, I love the roll-ing hills,

② I love the flow-ers, I love the daf-fo-dils,

③ I love the fire - side When all the lights are low.

Repeat until all parts join in

Boom-de-ah-da, boom-de-ah-da, Boom-de-

Ending

ah - da, boom - de - ay, Boom, boom, boom.

27

SHE'LL BE COMIN' ROUND THE MOUNTAIN

Traditional

1. She'll be com - in' round the moun - tain when she

comes, *Toot! Toot!* She'll be com - in' round the moun - tain
(pull train whistle)

when she comes, *Toot! Toot!* She'll be com - in' round the

moun-tain, She'll be com - in' round the moun-tain, She'll be

com - in' round the moun-tain when she comes. *Toot! Toot!*

2. She'll be drivin' six white horses when she comes.
   Whoa back! (pull on reins)
3. Oh, we'll all go out to greet her when she comes.
   Hi, there! (wave)
4. Then we'll all have chicken and dumplings when she comes.
   Yum, yum! (rub stomach)
5. Oh, she'll wear her red pajamas when she comes.
   Scratch, scratch! (scratch sides)
6. Oh, she'll have to sleep with Grandma when she comes.
   Snore, snore! (make snoring sound)

Action:

At the end of each verse, repeat the spoken part and actions of the previous verses in reverse order.

JOHN JACOB JINGLEHEIMER SCHMIDT

Traditional

John Ja - cob Jin - gle - heim - er Schmidt,

that's my name, too! When-ev-er I go out, the

peo - ple al-ways shout, "John Ja-cob Jin-gle-heim-er

Schmidt!" Da, da, da, da, da, da, da, da!

Action:

Repeat several times, each time softer until whispering, but always louder on the "da da . . . ."

TAKE ME OUT TO THE BALL GAME

Jack Norworth   *Albert von Tilzer*

Take me out to the ball game, Take me

out to the crowd,____ Buy me some

pea-nuts and Crack-er Jack, I don't care if I

nev-er come back, And it's root, root, root for the

home team, If they don't win, it's a shame,

For it's one, two, three strikes, "You're

out!" At the old ball game.____

TO MARKET, TO MARKET

1598

Traditional

1. To mar-ket, to mar-ket, to buy a fat pig;

Home a-gain, home a-gain, jig-get-y jig. To

mar-ket, to mar-ket, to buy a fat hog;

Home a-gain, home a-gain, jig-get-y jog.

2. To market, to market, to buy a white cake;
Home again, home again, never was baked.
To market, to market, to buy a plum bun;
Home again, home again, market is done.

THIS LITTLE PIG WENT TO MARKET

Traditional

This lit-tle pig went to mar-ket,
(wiggle child's big toe)

This lit-tle pig stayed at home,
(wiggle second toe)

This lit-tle pig had___ roast beef,
(wiggle third toe)

This lit-tle pig had___ none, And
(wiggle fourth toe)

this lit-tle pig cried, "Wee-wee-wee-wee-wee,"
(wiggle little toe)

All the way home.

OLD MACDONALD HAD A FARM

Traditional

1. Old Mac-Don-ald had a farm, E - I - E - I - O!

And on his farm he had some chicks, E - I - E - I - O!

With a ⒶChick, chick here, and a chick, chick there,

Here a chick, there a chick, ev-'ry-where a chick, chick,

Old Mac-Don-ald had a farm, E - I - E - I - O!

2. And on his farm he had some ducks, E-I-E-I-O!
   With a Ⓑquack, quack here, and a quack, quack there,
   Here a quack, there a quack, ev'rywhere a quack, quack,
   ⒶChick, chick here, and a chick, chick there,
   Here a chick, there a chick, ev'rywhere a chick, chick,
   Old MacDonald had a farm, E-I-E-I-O!

3. ... cow ... ©*moo, moo* ...

4. ... turkey ... [Ⓓ]*gobble, gobble* ...

Action:
Ⓐ Bob head
Ⓑ Flap elbows
Ⓒ Milk cow
Ⓓ Make turkey tail by hooking
   thumbs and spreading fingers

Suggestion:
Continue song by adding more animals (for example, pig ... oink,
oink [push up tip of nose], donkey ... hee-haw [hands up on head
to make ears] ....)

35

PEASE PORRIDGE HOT

Traditional

Pease por-ridge hot, Pease por-ridge cold,
(clap) *(clap)* *(spread arms)* *(clap)* *(clap)* *(spread arms)*

Pease por-ridge in the pot, Nine days old.
(clap) *(clap)* *(spread arms)* *(clap)* *(clap)* *(spread arms)*

Some like it hot, Some like it cold,
(continue as above)

Some like it in the pot, Nine days old.

Action:
- Infant—Hold on lap, guide hands in the movements.
- Toddler—For partner clapping game, face each other, clap own hands twice, clap partner's hands once. Continue throughout.
- Older—Slap own knees, clap own hands, clap partner's hands . . . .

PLAYMATE

Traditional

Say, say, oh, play-mate, come out and play with me,

And bring your dol-lies three, Climb up my ap-ple tree,

Cry down my rain barrel, Slide down my cel-lar door,

And we'll be jol-ly friends for-ev-er more.

Formation:
Partners are seated, facing each other.

Action 1:
- Begin on *play-* to do the following motions: slap knees, clap own hands, clap partner's hands, clap own hands.
- Repeat this sequence throughout the song.

Action 2: (For older children)
- *play*—slap knees twice
  mate—clap own hands twice
  (rest)—clap partner's hands once
  come—partners clap backs of
         hands together once
  out—clap partner's hands once
  and—clap own hands once
- Repeat this sequence in
  rhythm throughout the song.

MY AUNT CAME BACK

Traditional

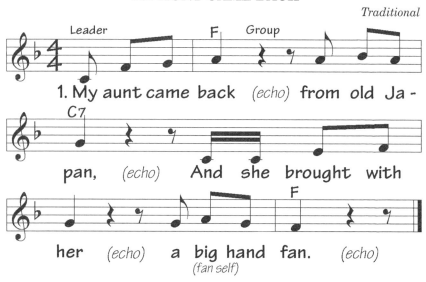

1. My aunt came back *(echo)* **from old Ja-pan,** *(echo)* **And she brought with her** *(echo)* **a big hand fan.** *(echo)*
(fan self)

2. **My aunt came back** *(echo)*
   (continue fanning)
   From old Algiers,
   And she brought with her . . .
   A pair of shears . . . .
   *(continue fanning with one hand,
   cut like scissors with fingers of
   the other hand)*

38

3. My aunt came back ...
   From Holland, too ...
   And she brought with her ...
   A wooden shoe ....
   *(continue previous actions,
   add stomping foot on floor)*

4. My aunt came back ...
   From Niagara Falls ...
   And she brought with her ...
   A ping-pong ball ....
   (add swinging head back and forth)

5. My aunt came back ...
   From the New York Fair ...
   And she brought with her ...
   A rocking chair ....
   (add rocking, as in a rocking chair)

6. My aunt came back ...
   From Kalamazoo ...
   And she brought with her ...
   Some gum to chew ....
   (add chewing)

7. My aunt came back ...
   From Timbuktu ...
   And she brought with her ...
   SOME CLOWNS LIKE YOU!
   (leader points to group)

Formation:
Children sit facing a leader.

Action:
- The leader sings alone, starting the action on the last phrase of the first verse.
- The group echoes each phrase and copies the actions of the leader.
- As new actions are added, children continue doing all previous actions at the same time.

TINGALAYO

Traditional West Indies

Tin-ga-lay-o! *(clap, clap)* Come, lit-tle don-key, come, —

Tin-ga-lay-o! *(clap, clap)* Come, lit-tle don-key, come. —

1. M' don-key walk, m' don-key talk, M' don-key

eat with a knife and fork, M' don-key walk, m'

don-key talk, M' don-key eat with a knife and fork.

2. M'donkey eat, m'donkey sleep,
   M'donkey kick with his two hind feet.
   M'donkey eat, m'donkey sleep,
   M'donkey kick with his two hind feet.
   Tingalayo! Come, little donkey, come,
   Tingalayo! Come, little donkey, come.

DOWN BY THE STATION
(Round)

Traditional

Down by the sta-tion, ear-ly in the morn-ing,

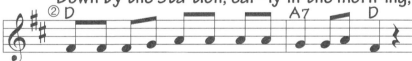

See the lit-tle puf-fer bel-lies all in a row,

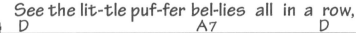

See the en-gine driv-er pull the lit-tle han-dle,

"Chug, Chug, Toot, Toot!" Off we go!

I'VE BEEN WORKING ON THE RAILROAD

American Work Song

I've been work-in' on the rail-road, All the live-long day,

I've been work-in' on the rail-road, Just to pass the time a-way,

Don't you hear the whis-tle blow-in', Rise up so ear-ly in the

morn; Don't you hear the cap-tain shout-ing, "Di-nah, blow your

horn!" Di-nah, won't you blow, Di-nah, won't you blow,

Di-nah, won't you blow your horn,___ Di-nah, won't you blow,

Di-nah, won't you blow, Di-nah, won't you blow your horn!

Some-one's in the kitch-en with Di-nah, Some-one's in the

kitch-en, I know,___ Some-one's in the kitch-en with Di-nah,

Strum-min' on the old ban-jo And sing-in', "Fee, Fi,

Fid-dlee-i-o, Fee, Fi, Fid-dlee-i-o,___ Fee, Fi,

Fid-dlee-i-o," Strum-min' on the old ban-jo.

TEN IN A BED

Traditional

1. There were ten in a bed and the lit-tle one

said, "Roll o - ver, roll o - ver." So they

all rolled o - ver and one fell out.

2. There were nine in a bed . . .

(Verses 3-9—Count one less each repetition)

10. There was one in the bed and the little one said, "*Good night.*"

44

THE FARMER IN THE DELL

Traditional

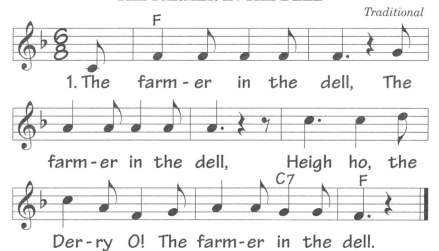

1. The farm-er in the dell, The farm-er in the dell, Heigh ho, the Der-ry O! The farm-er in the dell.

2. The farmer takes the wife . . .
3. The wife takes the child . . .
4. The child takes the nurse . . .
5. The nurse takes the dog . . .
6. The dog takes the cat . . .
7. The cat takes the rat . . .
8. The rat takes the cheese . . .
9. The cheese stands alone . . .

Formation:
Children stand in a circle, hands joined. One child, the *farmer*, stands in the center.

Action:
- Children circle around the *farmer*.
- On verse 2, the *farmer* chooses a *wife* to join him in the center of the circle.
- The game continues until the last verse, when all but the *cheese* return to the circle.
- The *cheese* becomes the *farmer* for the new game.

Suggestion:
Those inside the circle may circle around within the larger circle.

KOOKABURRA
(Round)

Traditional

1. Kook-a-bur-ra sits in the old gum tree, —

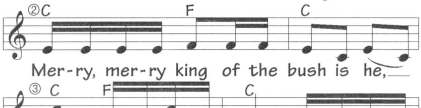

Mer-ry, mer-ry king of the bush is he, —

Laugh, Kook-a-bur-ra, laugh, Kook-a-bur-ra,

Gay your life must be.

2. Kookaburra sits in the old gum tree
   Eating all the gumdrops he can see,
   Stop, Kookaburra, stop, Kookaburra,
   Leave some there for me.

POP! GOES THE WEASEL

Traditional

All a-round the cob - bler's bench, The

mon - key chased the wea - sel. The

mon - key thought 'twas all___ in fun,

POP! goes the wea - sel.

Suggestions:
- Roll hands while singing. Clap on *POP*.
- Circle around, fall down on *POP*.
- Pass ball around circle. On *POP*, toss or roll ball across circle.

POLLY WOLLY DOODLE

Traditional

1. Oh, I went down South for to see my Sal, Sing
Pol-ly wol-ly doo-dle all the day, My Sal, she is a
spunk-y gal, Sing Pol-ly wol-ly doo-dle all the day.

Chorus

Fare thee well, fare thee well, Fare thee well my
fair-y fay, For I'm goin' to Lou'-si-an-a for to
see my Su-sy-an-na, Sing Pol-ly wol-ly doo-dle all the day.

2. Oh, my Sal, she is a maiden fair . . .
With curly eyes and laughing hair . . .

   (Chorus after each verse)

3. Behind the barn, down on my knees . . .
I thought I heard a chicken sneeze . . .

4. He sneezed so hard with the whooping cough . . .
He sneezed his head and tail right off . . .

5. Oh, a grasshopper sittin' on a railroad track . . .
   A-pickin' his teeth with a carpet tack . . .

6. Oh, I went to bed but it wasn't any use . . .
   My feet stuck out like a chicken roost . . .

Optional Descant   S.N.

F

1. Oh, I went down South to see my Sal, I'm

C7

sing-ing all the way, My__ Sal, she is a

F

spunk-y gal, I'm sing-ing all the day.

Chorus
F

Fare thee well,   fare thee well,

C7

Fare thee well, I say,   Fare thee well,

F

fare thee well, Sing-ing all the day.

49

HICKORY, DICKORY, DOCK

England, 1744   *Traditional*

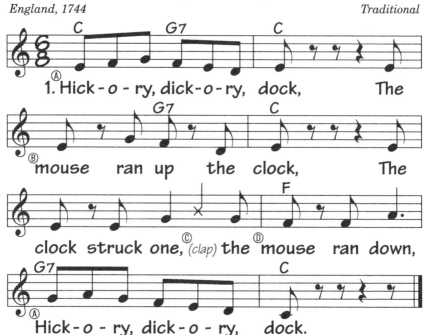

1. Hick-o-ry, dick-o-ry, dock, The
mouse ran up the clock, The
clock struck one, (clap) the mouse ran down,
Hick-o-ry, dick-o-ry, dock.

2. ⒶHickory, Dickory, Dock,
   The ⒷMouse ran up the clock,
   The clock struck two,Ⓒ *(clap, clap)*
   The mouse said, Ⓔ"Boo!"
   ⒶHickory, dickory, dock.

3. ...The clock struck three...
   The mouse said, Ⓕ"Whee!" ...

4. ...The clock struck four...
   The mouse said, Ⓖ"No more!" ...

Action:
Ⓐ Hands in praying position,
   rock them left to right
Ⓑ Wiggle fingers upward
Ⓒ Clap hands above head
Ⓓ Wiggle fingers downward
Ⓔ Hands around mouth
Ⓕ Hands up in surprise
Ⓖ Shake head no

50

RING AROUND THE ROSY

England, 1665

Ring a-round the ros - y, A pock-et

full of po - sies, Ash - es,

ash - es, We all fall DOWN!

Formation:
Children stand in a circle, hands joined.

Action:
Children circle around and fall down on the last word. Repeat,
faster each time.

Suggestion:
Try different actions while circling (for example, tiptoe round the
rosy, skip, hop, run . . . .)

51

THE HOKEY POKEY

Traditional

1. You put your right hand in, you put your right hand out,

You put your right hand in, and you shake it all a-

bout, You do the ho-key po-key, and you

(bend elbows, point index fingers up, sway hips)

turn your-self a-round, That's what it's all a-bout!

(clap in rhythm)

2. You put your left hand in . . .
3. . . . right foot in . . .
4. . . . left foot in . . .
5. . . . right shoulder in . . .
6. . . . left shoulder in . . .
7. . . . right hip in . . .
8. . . . left hip in . . .
9. . . . head in . . .
10. . . . whole self in . . .

Formation:
Children stand in a circle.

Action:
Follow the actions of the words.

TEDDY BEAR

Traditional

1. Ted-dy Bear, Ted-dy Bear, turn a-round,

Ted-dy Bear, Ted-dy Bear, touch the ground,

Ted-dy Bear, Ted-dy Bear, show your shoe,

Ted-dy Bear, Ted-dy Bear, that will do!

2. Teddy Bear, Teddy Bear, go upstairs,
   Teddy Bear, Teddy Bear, say your prayers,
   Teddy Bear, Teddy Bear, switch off the light,
   Teddy Bear, Teddy Bear, say, "Good-night."

Suggestion:
Do actions suggested by the words.

53

WHO BUILT THE ARK?

Spiritual

Chorus

F Solo — Who built the ark? C7 Group — No-ah! No-ah!

F Solo — Who built the ark? Group — Broth-er No-ah built the ark. C7 — F Fine

Verse

C Solo — 1. Old man No-ah built the ark,— He built it out of the hick-o-ry bark.— G7 ... C — He built it long, both wide and tall,—

With plen-ty of room for the large— and small.— G7 ... C — D.C. al fine

2. In came the animals, two by two,
   Hippopotamus and kangaroo.
   In came the animals, three by three,
   Two big cats and a bumblebee.

   (Chorus after each verse)

3. In came the animals, four by four,
   Two through the window and two through the door.
   In came the animals, five by five,
   The bees came swarming from the hive.

4. In came the animals, six by six,
   Elephant laughed at the monkey's tricks.
   In came the animals, seven by seven,
   Giraffes and the camels looking up to heaven.

5. In came the animals, eight by eight,
   Some on time and the others were late.
   In came the animals, nine by nine,
   Some were laughin' and some were cryin'.

6. In came the animals, ten by ten,
   Time for the voyage to begin.
   Noah said, "Go shut the door,
   The rain's started fallin' and we can't take more."

RAIN, RAIN, GO AWAY

Traditional

Rain, rain, go a-way, Come a-gain an-oth-er day,

Lit-tle Bet-ty wants to play, Rain,＿ rain,＿ go a-way.
(any name)

THERE IS THUNDER
(Tune: Are You Sleeping?)
Round

Traditional

Ⓐ There is thun-der, there is thun-der,

Hear it roar, hear it roar.

Ⓑ Pit-ter, pat-ter rain-drops, pit-ter, pat-ter

rain-drops, Ⓒ I'm all wet. I'm all wet.

Action:
Ⓐ Slap floor with palms of hands alternately and quickly
Ⓑ Slap thighs in same way
Ⓒ Shake rain off hands

IT'S RAINING

(Tune: Rain, Rain Go Away)

Traditional

It's rain - ing, it's pour-ing, The old man is

snor-ing, He went to bed and bumped his head And

could - n't get up in the morn - ing.

SING-A-LING

Traditional

Oh, my dear friend, I sing-a-ling-a-ling with all my heart to you; I hope there'll be some-thing-a-ling-a-ling that I can do for you. In au-tumn, win-ter, spring-a-ling-a-ling, and all the whole year through, I'll ring-a-ling-a-ling, and ting-a-ling-a-ling, and sing-a-ling-a-ling for you.

Suggestion:
Insert names of family members, friends, etc.

HE'S GOT THE WHOLE WORLD

Traditional

1. He's got the whole world__ in His hands,__ He's got the whole world__ in His hands,__ He's got the whole world__ in His hands,__ He's got the whole world in His hands.

2. He's got the little, bitty baby in His hands,
   He's got the little, bitty baby in His hands,
   He's got the little, bitty baby in His hands,
   He's got the whole world in His hands.

3. He's got you and me, brother . . .

4. He's got you and me, sister . . .

5. He's got everybody here . . .

6. He's got the wind and the rain . . .

7. He's got the sun and the moon . . .

8. He's got the whole world . . .

HUSH, LITTLE BABY

Southern U.S.

1. Hush, lit-tle ba-by, don't say a word,

Pa-pa's gon-na buy you a mock-ing-bird.

2. If that mockingbird don't sing,
   Papa's gonna buy you a diamond ring.

3. If that diamond ring turns brass,
   Papa's gonna buy you a looking glass.

4. If that looking glass gets broke,
   Papa's gonna buy you a billy goat.

5. If that billy goat don't pull,
   Papa's gonna buy you a cart and bull.

6. If that cart and bull turn over,
   Papa's gonna buy you a dog named Rover.

7. If that dog named Rover don't bark,
   Papa's gonna buy you a horse and cart.

8. If that horse and cart fall down,
   You'll still be the sweetest little baby in town.

60

TWINKLE, TWINKLE, LITTLE STAR

Jane Taylor, 1806   *Traditional*

1. Twin-kle, twin-kle, lit-tle star, How I won-der what you are, Up a-bove the world so high, Like a dia-mond in the sky, Twin-kle, twin-kle, lit-tle star, How I won-der what you are.

2. When the blazing sun is gone,
   When he nothing shines upon,
   Then you show your little light,
   Twinkle, twinkle, all the night,
   Twinkle, twinkle, little star,
   How I wonder what you are.

3. Then the traveler in the dark,
   Thanks you for your tiny spark,
   He could not see where to go,
   If you did not twinkle so,
   Twinkle, twinkle, little star,
   How I wonder what you are.

4. In the dark blue sky you keep,
   Often through my curtains peep,
   For you never shut your eye,
   Till the sun is in the sky,
   Twinkle, twinkle, little star,
   How I wonder what you are.

INDEX

Ants Go Marching, The 24
Baby Bumblebee 23
Bear Went Over the Mountain, The 26
Big Rock Candy Mountains, The 12
Bingo 10
Do Your Ears Hang Low? 11
Down by the Bay 14
Down by the Station 41
Dry Bones 18
Eentsy, Weentsy Spider 22
Farmer in the Dell, The 45
Head and Shoulders 17
He's Got the Whole World 59
Hickory, Dickory, Dock 50
Hokey Pokey, The 52
Hush, Little Baby 60
I Love the Mountains 27
If You're Happy 7
It's Raining 57
I've Been Working on the Railroad 42
John Jacob Jingleheimer Schmidt 30
Kookaburra 46
Looby Loo 20
More Wee Sing Together, The 6
My Aunt Came Back 38
Old MacDonald Had a Farm 34
Pease Porridge Hot 36
Playmate 37
Polly Wolly Doodle 48
Pop! Goes the Weasel 47
Rain, Rain, Go Away 56
Ring Around the Rosy 51
Row, Row, Row Your Boat 16
She'll Be Comin' Round the Mountain 28
Sing-a-ling 58
Six Little Ducks 15
Skidamarink 8
Take Me Out to the Ball Game 31

Teddy Bear 53
Ten in a Bed 44
There Is Thunder 56
This Little Pig Went to Market 33
Tingalayo 40
To Market, to Market 32
Twinkle, Twinkle, Little Star 61
Who Built the Ark? 54